AC 11394

594
B

D

AC 11394

RAINY DAYS

CHRISTMAS

DENNY ROBSON

GLOUCESTER PRESS
New York · London · Toronto · Sydney

CONTENTS

Design: David West
                Children's Book Design
Designer: Flick Killerby
Photography: Roger Vlitos

© Aladdin Books Ltd 1992

*First published in
the United States in 1992 by*
Gloucester Press
95 Madison Avenue
New York, NY 10016

Library of Congress
Cataloging-in-Publication Data

Robson, Denny.
      Christmas / by Denny A. Robson.
        p. cm. — (Rainy days)
      Includes index.
      Summary: Examines traditional Christmas
activities, discussing tree ornaments, holiday
cards, gift wrap, bows, Advent calendars, and
Nativity scenes.
      ISBN 0-531-17333-X
      1. Christmas decorations—Juvenile
literature. [1. Christmas decorations. 2.
Handicrafts.] I. Title. II. Series.
TT900.C4R6   1992
745.594'12—dc20   92-3214   CIP   AC

Printed in Belgium

Introduction

Christmas is an exciting time — nativity plays at school, carol services to celebrate the birth of Jesus, trees to decorate, stockings to be hung up, cards and presents to be exchanged, as well as all the fun to be had with your friends and family.

You can also have a lot of fun with the preparations, and this book is full of ideas to help you get ready for Christmas. There are cards for you to make, an advent calendar, hanging decorations, baubles for the tree, wrapping papers, and even a nativity scene.

Some of the ideas are simple and can be made quite quickly. Others will take more time and you may need the help of an older person. But they are all great fun and they should get you into the festive spirit!

Here are some of the materials used to make the projects in this book. Most things are not expensive to buy and you may find much of what you need at home. (This Christmas, remember to save a few cards to be used in your preparations for next year.) Before you begin, check the materials needed and gather everything together. It's also a good idea to cover your work surface with newspaper before you begin.

Christmas cards

Your Christmas greetings to friends and family will be even more special if you send them on homemade cards. Try these designs and then see if you can make up others of your own.

You will need thin cardboard, scissors, felttip pens, colored tissue paper, foil, glitter, glue, gummed stars.

1 To make the snowman and stocking, fold the cardboard, draw the shapes and cut them out from the fold so that the shapes are double. Draw the robin on single cardboard and cut out.

1

2 Decorate your
cards as shown.
When using glitter, first
fold and unfold a piece of
paper and place this
under the card. You can
then refold the paper and
pour any excess glitter
back into the tube.

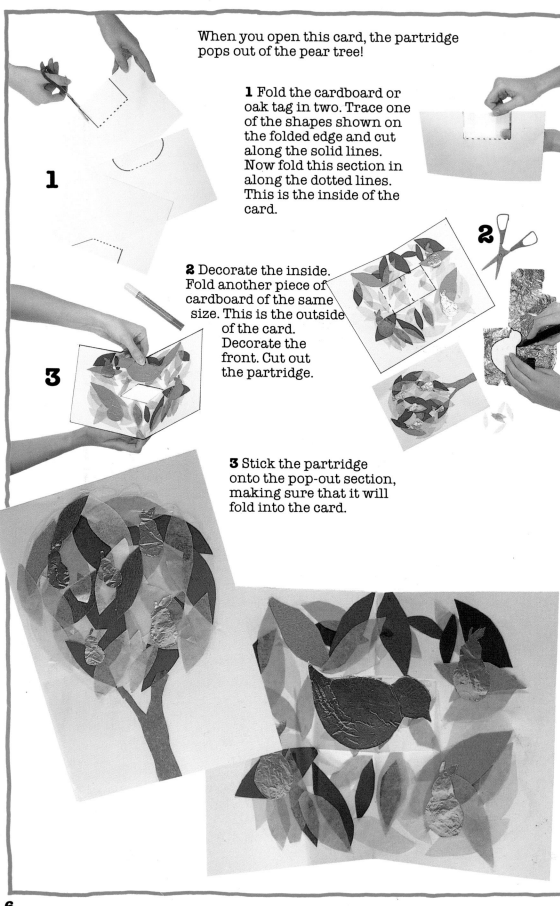

When you open this card, the partridge pops out of the pear tree!

1 Fold the cardboard or oak tag in two. Trace one of the shapes shown on the folded edge and cut along the solid lines. Now fold this section in along the dotted lines. This is the inside of the card.

2 Decorate the inside. Fold another piece of cardboard of the same size. This is the outside of the card. Decorate the front. Cut out the partridge.

3 Stick the partridge onto the pop-out section, making sure that it will fold into the card.

In this card, Santa's sleigh flies through the night sky, leaving a trail of stars.

1 Take three pieces of cardboard or oak tag the same size. Paint two blue as shown. Cut a window in the top piece and stick a trail of stars to the base in the same position.

2 Draw your Santa on a strip of cardboard a little longer than the window.

3 Trace the window onto the third piece of cardboard. Cut it out to one edge and glue to the base piece. This acts as a runner to keep Santa in place.

4 Slide the strip into the base.

5 Glue the top to the base.

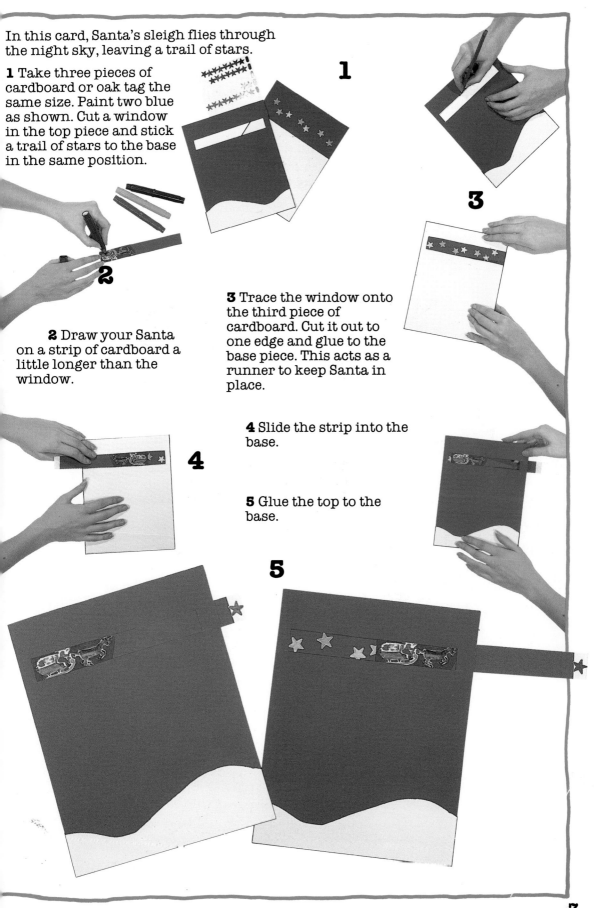

Garlands

Paper chains and garlands are very traditional Christmas decorations. They can be hung diagonally across a room, or strung along the walls to make your home look festive. They can be as long as you want, (unlike the ones in the stores!), and are very simple to make.

You will need colored paper, pencil, ruler, scissors, stapler, glue.

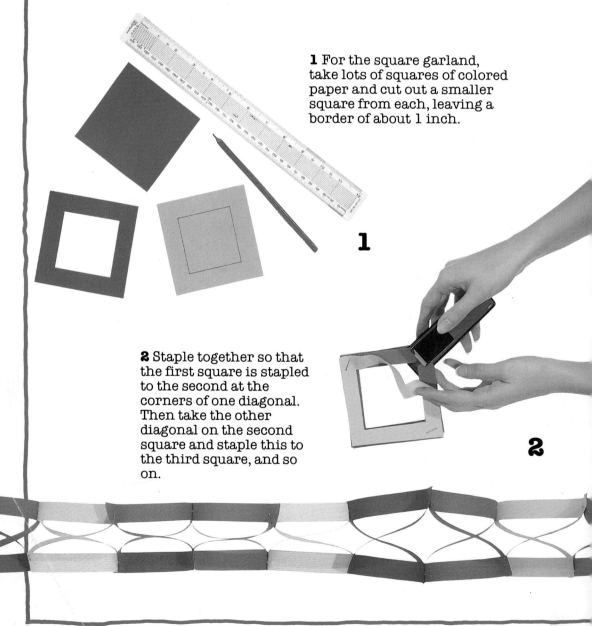

1 For the square garland, take lots of squares of colored paper and cut out a smaller square from each, leaving a border of about 1 inch.

1

2 Staple together so that the first square is stapled to the second at the corners of one diagonal. Then take the other diagonal on the second square and staple this to the third square, and so on.

2

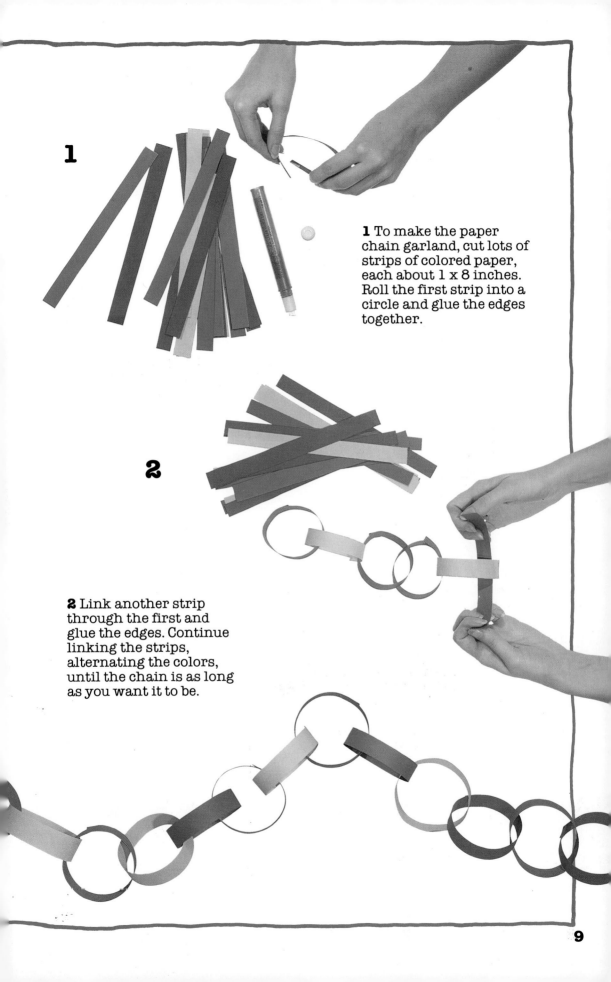

1

1 To make the paper chain garland, cut lots of strips of colored paper, each about 1 x 8 inches. Roll the first strip into a circle and glue the edges together.

2

2 Link another strip through the first and glue the edges. Continue linking the strips, alternating the colors, until the chain is as long as you want it to be.

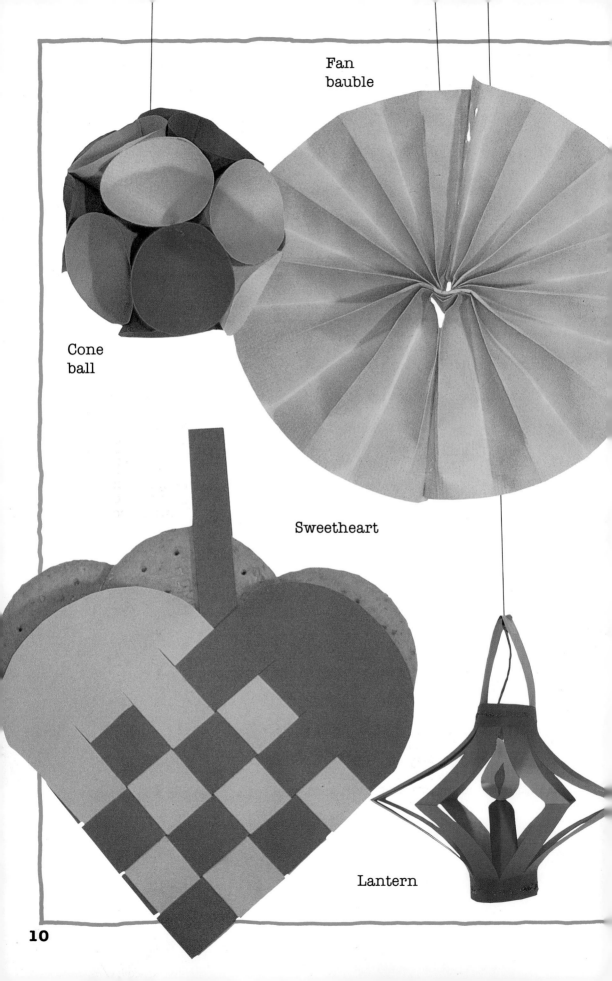

Fan
bauble

Cone
ball

Sweetheart

Lantern

Tree decorations

For many people, Christmas wouldn't be Christmas without a tree decorated with tiny lights, tinsel, and baubles. Here are some ideas for decorations that could be hung from the tree, or from the ceiling. Decorate with paints or glitter to make them even more special. You can find out how to make an angel to go on top of the tree on page 30.

You will need colored paper, glue, glitter, cookies or candy to put in the sweet-heart basket, ribbon or string for hanging.

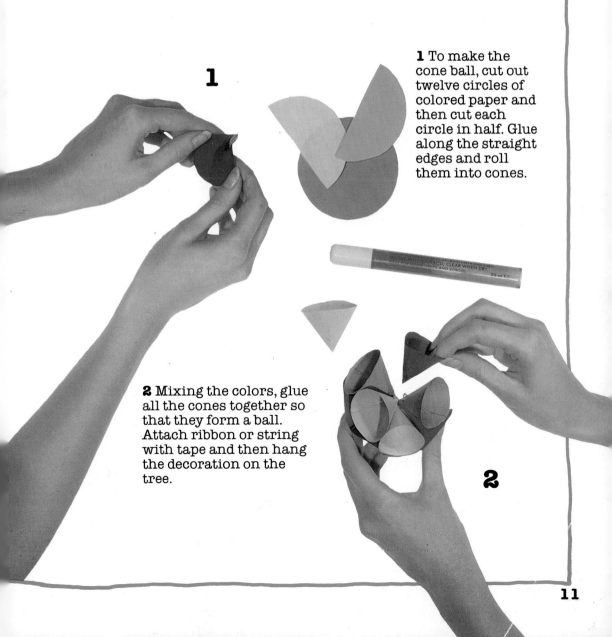

1

1 To make the cone ball, cut out twelve circles of colored paper and then cut each circle in half. Glue along the straight edges and roll them into cones.

2 Mixing the colors, glue all the cones together so that they form a ball. Attach ribbon or string with tape and then hang the decoration on the tree.

2

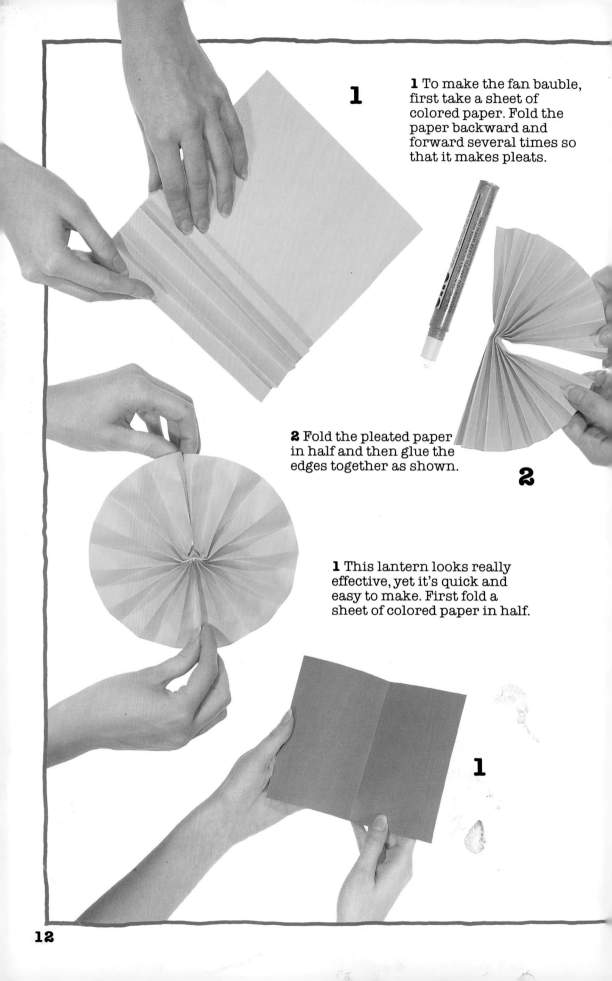

1 To make the fan bauble, first take a sheet of colored paper. Fold the paper backward and forward several times so that it makes pleats.

2 Fold the pleated paper in half and then glue the edges together as shown.

1 This lantern looks really effective, yet it's quick and easy to make. First fold a sheet of colored paper in half.

1 To make the sweetheart, take two pieces of paper 2½ by 8 inches of different colors. Fold in half across the width and cut a curve opposite the fold. Make three cuts from the fold as shown.

1

2 Interweave the two parts together and the heart will open out to make a basket.

2

3

2 Make cuts along the folded edge.

3 Open out and glue along the two long sides.

4 Glue a paper strip to your lantern to make a handle. Cut out the paper candle and attach it to the handle using tape and string.

2

4

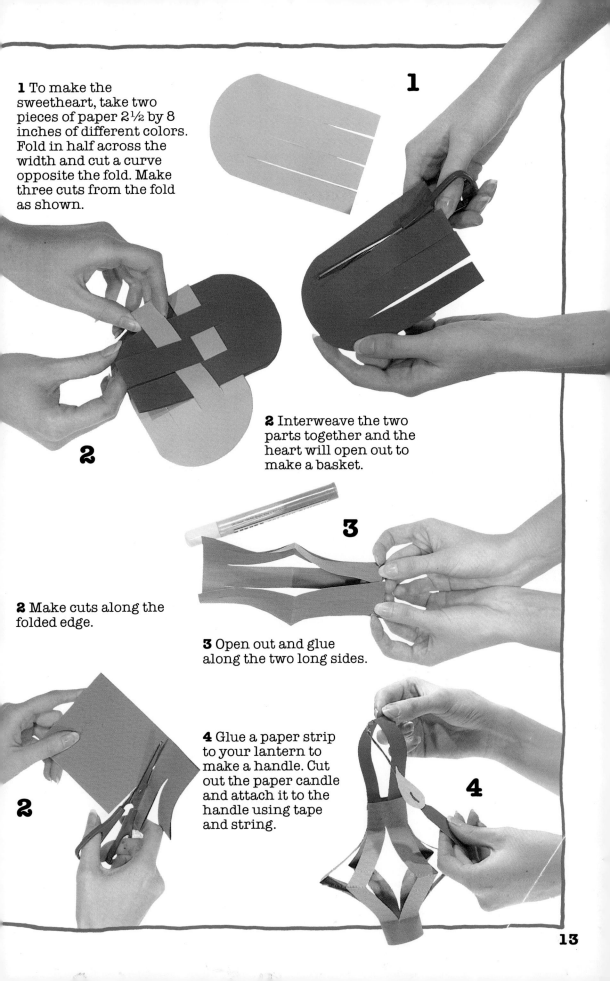

13

"Stained-glass" picture

Have you noticed the stained-glass windows in some churches? Here is an idea for a "stained-glass" Christmas picture for you to make. The design can be as simple as you like — a big star or an arched window, for example. Or you can trace a picture with lots of detail, like this decorated Christmas tree and presents. When it's finished, hang your picture up against a window so that the light shines through the colored paper.

You will need black cardboard, pencil, colored tissue paper, tracing paper for more detailed designs, glue, scissors.

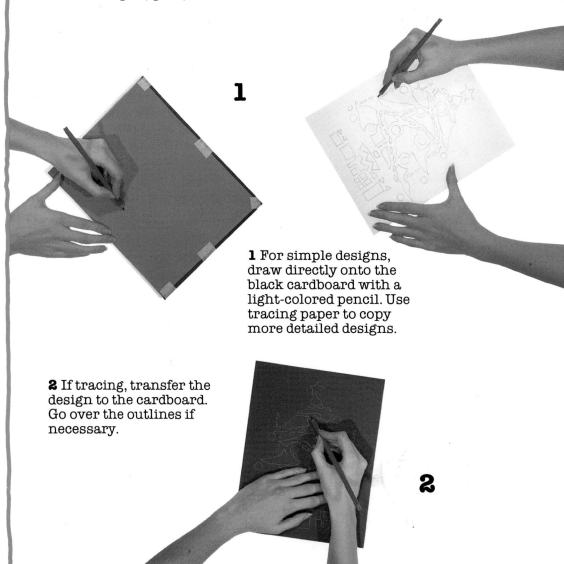

1

1 For simple designs, draw directly onto the black cardboard with a light-colored pencil. Use tracing paper to copy more detailed designs.

2 If tracing, transfer the design to the cardboard. Go over the outlines if necessary.

2

3

3 Carefully cut out the shapes. You may need the help of an adult. Make sure that the cardboard between the spaces is not too thin or it will tear.

4

4 Glue colored tissue to one side of the cardboard so that the cut out shapes are completely covered.

Advent calendar

Count down the days to Christmas with this advent calendar. Behind each "window" draw a Christmas picture — an angel, star, Christmas tree, presents, baubles, holly or a snowman, for example. For December 24, you could make a bigger window and draw the baby Jesus in a manger. Open the first window on December 1 and continue opening a window each day until you get to Christmas Day. Then pull Santa down the chimney!

You will need cardboard, tracing paper, paints or felttip pens, black paper, glue.

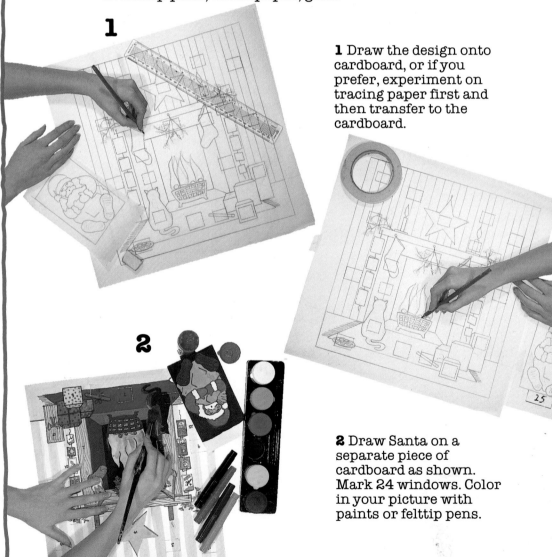

1

1 Draw the design onto cardboard, or if you prefer, experiment on tracing paper first and then transfer to the cardboard.

2

2 Draw Santa on a separate piece of cardboard as shown. Mark 24 windows. Color in your picture with paints or felttip pens.

3 Cut out three sides of each window. Glue the edges of the picture to a piece of cardboard of the same size. Draw small pictures behind each window.

3

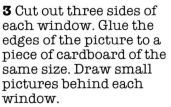

4

4 Cut a slit along the chimney through both pieces of cardboard. Push Santa up the chimney.

5

5 Turn the picture over and glue a piece of cardboard around Santa to keep him in place.

Glue   Back of Santa

6

6 When all the windows have been opened and it's Christmas Day, pull Santa down the chimney!

Christmas crackers

Crackers for the dinner table can make your Christmas meals begin with a bang! Here is a design for a very easy cracker to make yourself. You can fill it with anything you want, candy, small toys, party hats, jokes, or fortunes. Make each one different for the different members of your family. Decorate the crackers with small pictures cut from old Christmas cards.

You will need colored tissue paper, colored crêpe paper, a cardboard tube for each cracker, candy or small toys, jokes or fortunes, glue, scissors.

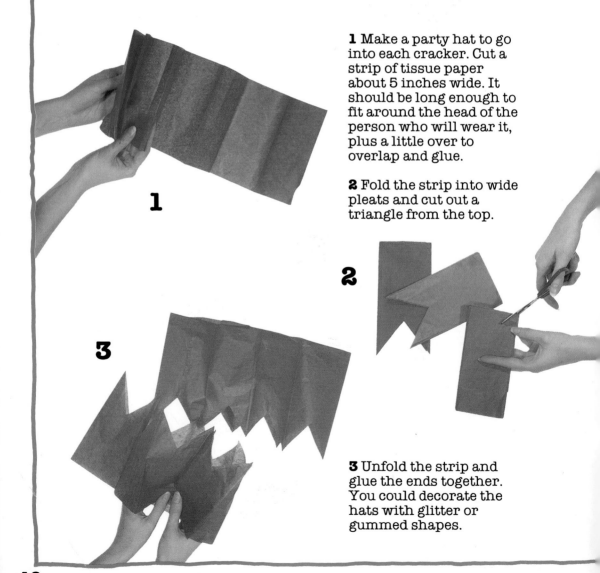

1 Make a party hat to go into each cracker. Cut a strip of tissue paper about 5 inches wide. It should be long enough to fit around the head of the person who will wear it, plus a little over to overlap and glue.

2 Fold the strip into wide pleats and cut out a triangle from the top.

3 Unfold the strip and glue the ends together. You could decorate the hats with glitter or gummed shapes.

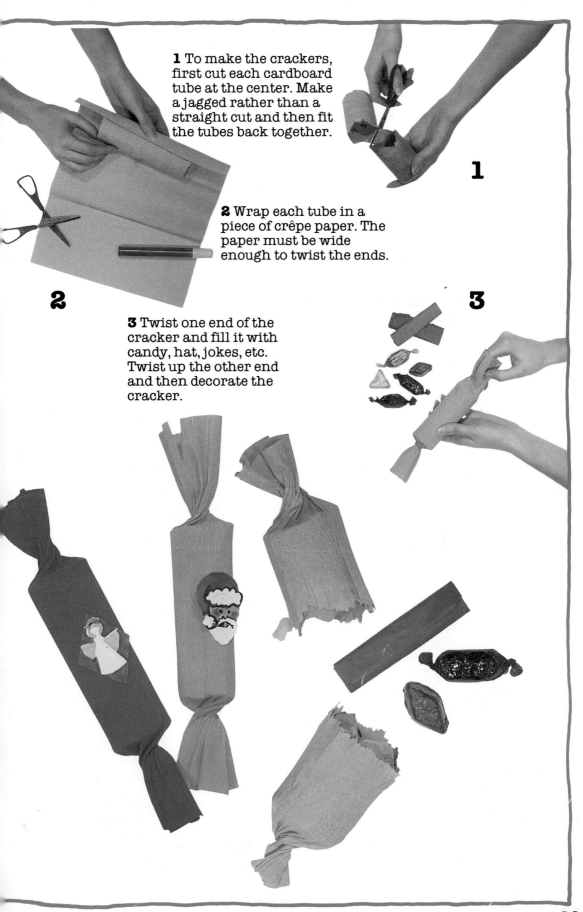

1 To make the crackers, first cut each cardboard tube at the center. Make a jagged rather than a straight cut and then fit the tubes back together.

1

2 Wrap each tube in a piece of crêpe paper. The paper must be wide enough to twist the ends.

2

3

3 Twist one end of the cracker and fill it with candy, hat, jokes, etc. Twist up the other end and then decorate the cracker.

Wrapping paper

Giving and receiving presents is one of the nicest things about Christmas, and your presents will look even more special if you make your own wrapping paper. Here are two kinds of paper for you to make: one patterned with potato prints and the other marbled. Use poster paint for the prints, but for the marbled paper you will need to use oil paints thinned with turpentine.

You will need large sheets of plain paper, poster paints, oil paints thinned with turpentine, (ask an adult to help), potatoes, felttip pen, knife, bowl of water.

1 Cut the potatoes in half.

2 Draw a simple design onto the cut surfaces of each potato.

3 Carefully cut around each design so that it stands out. You may need the help of an adult for this.

4 Dip the potato shapes into poster paints and print all over the paper. Leave it to dry.

1 Pour different colored oil paints (thinned) onto a bowl of water. The paint should float. Swirl the colors together.

2 Carefully lay a sheet of paper onto the surface of the water.

3 Peel off carefully and allow to dry.

Snowflake mobile

This snowflake mobile looks pretty hanging in the hall or stairwell where it can catch the air movements. You may have to experiment when putting it all together so that it hangs balanced. Real snowflake crystals all have six points, but you can make your snowflakes as varied as you like. They also make pretty decorations if you stick them to the windows.

You will need squares of paper for the snowflakes, thin cardboard or oak tag for the cloud, cotton balls, thread, scissors, tape, glue.

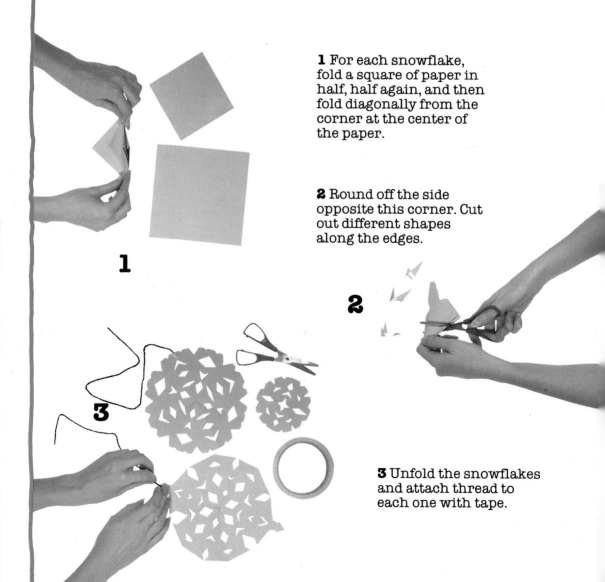

1 For each snowflake, fold a square of paper in half, half again, and then fold diagonally from the corner at the center of the paper.

2 Round off the side opposite this corner. Cut out different shapes along the edges.

3 Unfold the snowflakes and attach thread to each one with tape.

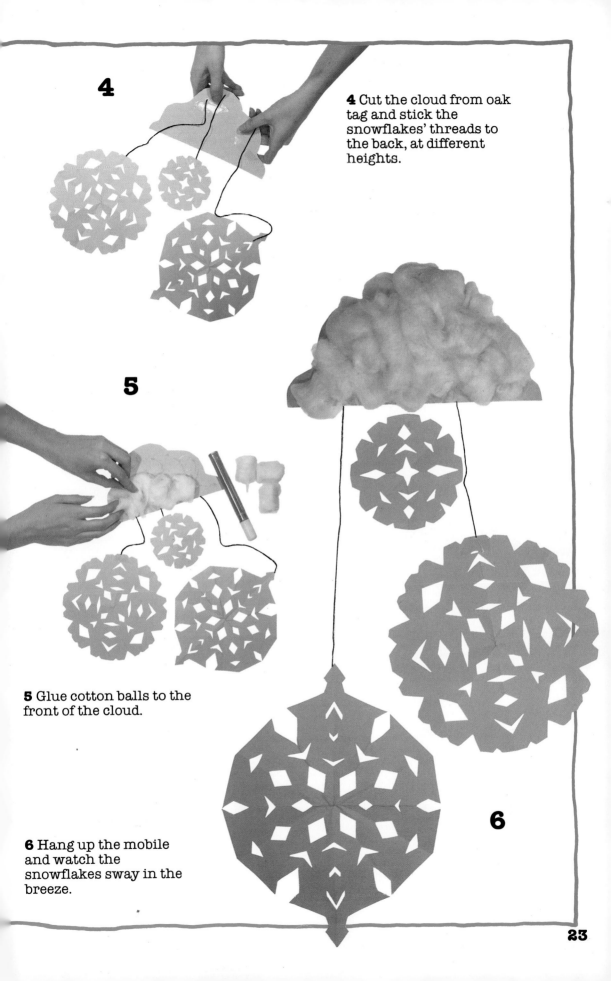

4

4 Cut the cloud from oak tag and stick the snowflakes' threads to the back, at different heights.

5

5 Glue cotton balls to the front of the cloud.

6 Hang up the mobile and watch the snowflakes sway in the breeze.

6

Snowstorm

Even if you have no snow at Christmas, you can still create your own snowstorm in a jar. This carol singer caught in the snow is fun to make. You could design lots of different characters and give them as presents to your friends.

You will need a glass jar with a tight-fitting lid, water, tinsel or aluminum foil for the snow, different colored modeling clay, a pencil.

1 Make the carol singer's body from clay. Give him a scarf and two arms. Fix two mittens to his book of carols and attach to his arms.

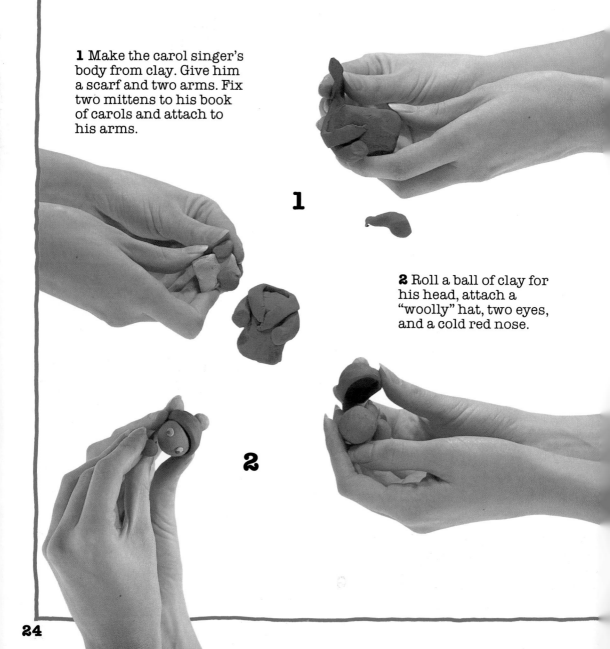

2 Roll a ball of clay for his head, attach a "woolly" hat, two eyes, and a cold red nose.

3 Use the point of a pencil to make his singing mouth.

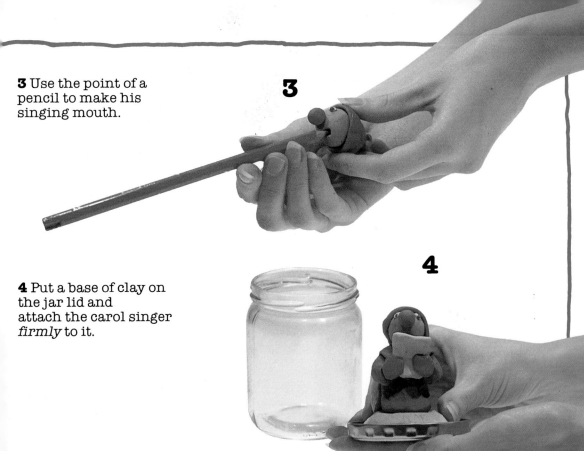

4 Put a base of clay on the jar lid and attach the carol singer *firmly* to it.

5 Fill the jar with water and add strands cut from a piece of tinsel, or tiny pieces of aluminum foil. Screw on the lid tightly and shake the jar to see the snow swirl.

Gift boxes

Here are some pretty Christmas gift boxes for you to make. You can make them any size you like and fill them with candy or presents to give to your friends and family. Decorate them with glitter, gummed shapes and pictures, or you can print them with the potato cuts as you did with the wrapping paper. The design for each box is on page 32.

You will need oak tag, pencil and ruler, glue, glitter, gummed shapes, paints or potato shapes to decorate.

1 Copy shape 1 shown on page 32 with a pencil and ruler. Draw in the dotted lines and cut along the solid lines. The box can be as large as you like, but you may need the help of an adult to work out the size.

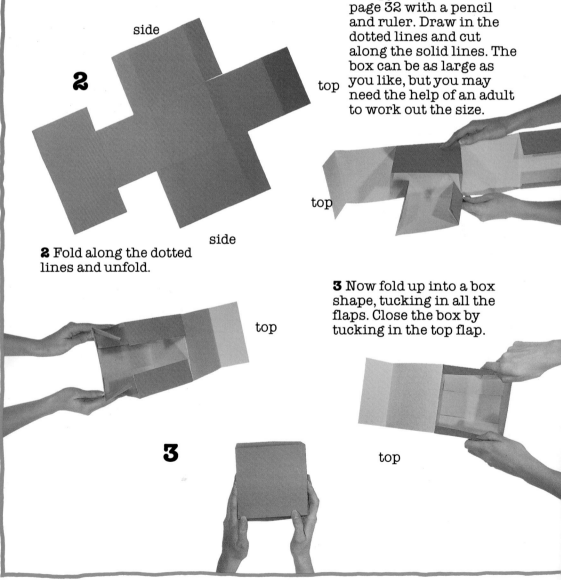

side

top

2

side

2 Fold along the dotted lines and unfold.

top

top

3 Now fold up into a box shape, tucking in all the flaps. Close the box by tucking in the top flap.

top

3

top

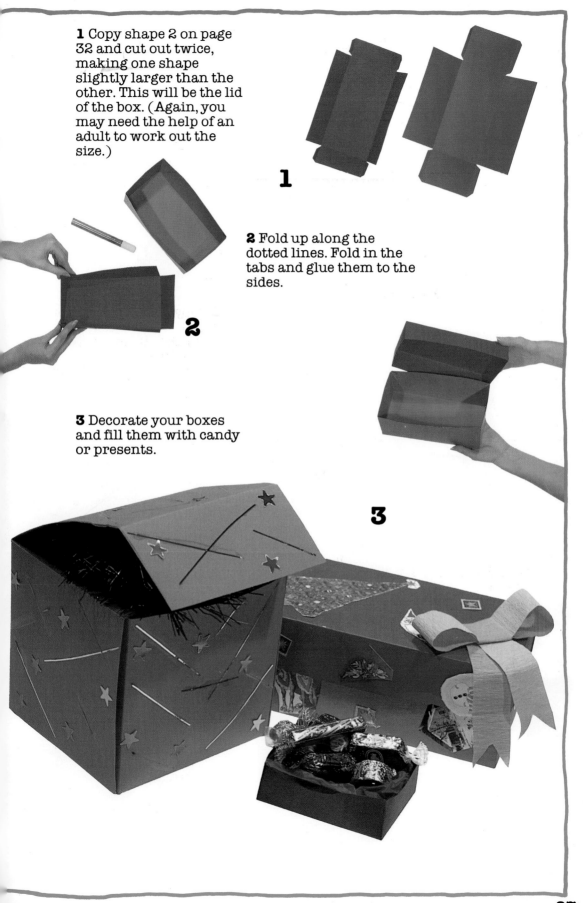

1 Copy shape 2 on page 32 and cut out twice, making one shape slightly larger than the other. This will be the lid of the box. (Again, you may need the help of an adult to work out the size.)

1

2 Fold up along the dotted lines. Fold in the tabs and glue them to the sides.

2

3 Decorate your boxes and fill them with candy or presents.

3

Nativity scene

Here are some ideas for a nativity scene for you to make. A bright new star twinkles in the sky above the stable where Jesus has just been born. Mary and Joseph stand beside him in the stable. An angel has appeared to tell the shepherds about Jesus' birth and they have come to visit. Three kings have also followed the star, bringing gifts for the baby Jesus.

You will need

cardboard, a shoe box, a matchbox for the crib, straw or yellow yarn, gold foil, gummed stars, paints and paintbrush, tissue and crêpe paper, cotton balls, pipe cleaners, modeling clay, tinsel, glue, thread spool.

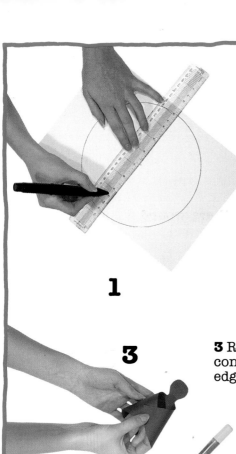

1 Draw a circle on cardboard using a plate or saucer. (Do this for as many characters as you need.) Draw a line through the middle.

1

2

2 Using a thread spool, draw the head as shown. Cut out the semi-circle with head.

3

3 Roll each body into a cone shape. Glue the edges together.

Angel

4 The angel has a tunic and arms made of white paper, and a gold foil halo and wings.

4

5 Glue semicircles of tissue paper or crêpe paper around the figures to make the clothes. Attach cardboard arms.

5

6 Decorate the figures as you like. The three kings can have tinsel or glitter crowns.

6

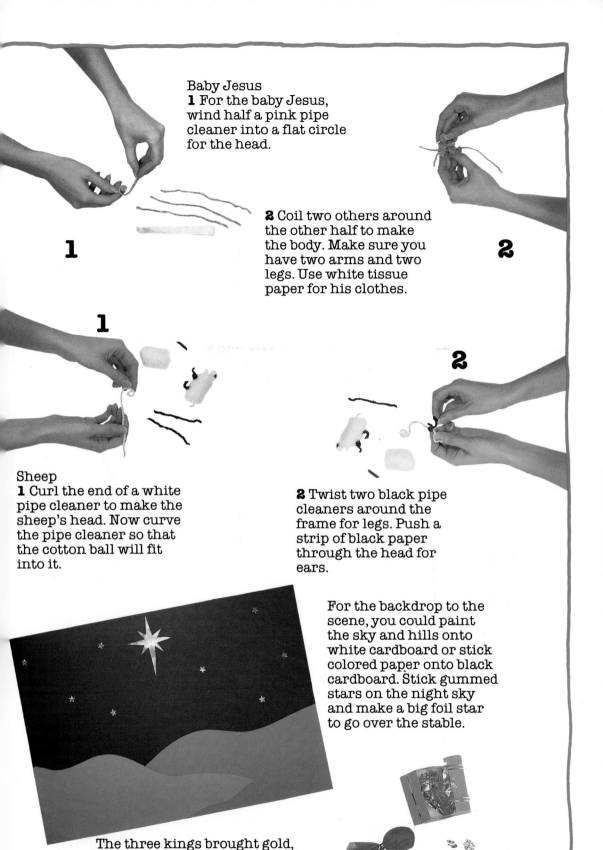

Baby Jesus
1 For the baby Jesus, wind half a pink pipe cleaner into a flat circle for the head.

1

2 Coil two others around the other half to make the body. Make sure you have two arms and two legs. Use white tissue paper for his clothes.

2

1

2

Sheep
1 Curl the end of a white pipe cleaner to make the sheep's head. Now curve the pipe cleaner so that the cotton ball will fit into it.

2 Twist two black pipe cleaners around the frame for legs. Push a strip of black paper through the head for ears.

For the backdrop to the scene, you could paint the sky and hills onto white cardboard or stick colored paper onto black cardboard. Stick gummed stars on the night sky and make a big foil star to go over the stable.

The three kings brought gold, frankincense, and myrrh. Wrap clay in scraps of fabric and tie with tinsel, and make a "chest" of gold foil as your gifts.

Gift box designs

Copy these designs to make the Christmas gift boxes on page 26. The boxes can be made to any size you wish. You may need the help of a grownup to calculate the scale.

1

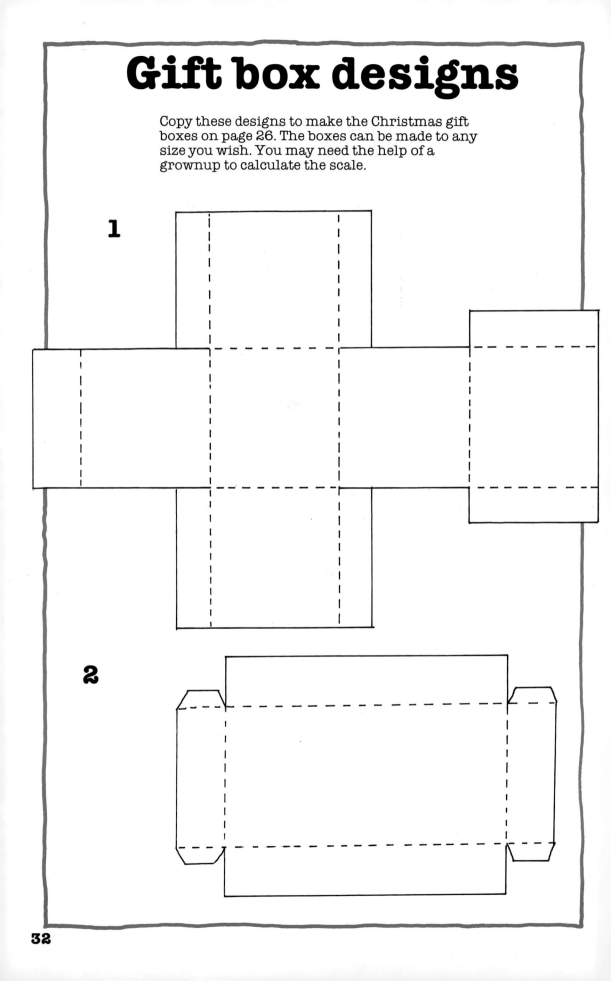

2